D0343178

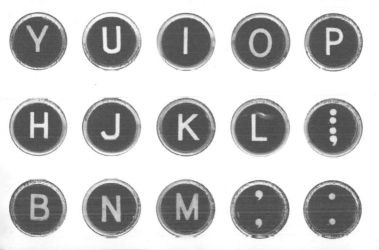

THIS BOOK BELONGS TO:

IF FOUND, REWARD OF _____.

OTHER TITLES IN
THE LITTLE BOOKS SERIES:

THE LITTLE BOOK
OF BOOKS

Jennifer Worick

CIDER MILL
PRESS

BOOK
PUBLISHERS

Kennebunkport, Maine

13-Digit ISBN: 1-60433-285-9
10-Digit ISBN: 978-1-60433-285-8

This book may be ordered by mail from the publisher.
Please include $2.95 for postage and handling.
Please support your local bookseller first!

Books published by Cider Mill Press Book Publishers are available at special discounts for bulk purchases in the United States by corporations, institutions, and other organizations. For more information, please contact the publisher.

Cider Mill Press Book Publishers
"Where good books are ready for press"
12 Port Farm Road
Kennebunkport, Maine 04046

Visit us on the Web!
www.cidermillpress.com

Design by Alicia Freile, Tango Media
Typography: Bodoni, Futura, Gill Sans and Love Letter Typewriter
Typewriter keys illustration courtesy of Robyn Mackenzie and used under license from Shutterstock.com

Printed in China

1 2 3 4 5 6 7 8 9 0
First Edition

SLIP BETWEEN
THE SHEETS

It was the best of times, it was the worst of times...

But even during the darkest of days, we find comfort in books. The enduring power of reading has energized, enraged, inspired revolutions, broken hearts, and saved lives. From their earliest beginnings on papyrus and parchment to today's ever-evolving landscape of e-readers and unconventional formats, books have managed to mirror the times and predict the future (Big Brother, I'm looking at you here). They've been handed down through generations as prized possessions, and they've been pressed furtively into hands to spread dangerous, thrilling knowledge that seemed like *Common Sense* at the time.

There have certainly been some low points as well. The power of books is so great, potentially so threatening, that they've been banned and even—*gasp!*—burned to destroy opposing viewpoints. Clearly—and happily, I must add—things didn't exactly go as planned. Books, like life itself, will find a way (now I'm shamelessly cribbing from *Jurassic Park*).

As long as there are readers, there will be books, no matter what form they may take.

My lifelong love affair with the printed word started at a young age. Growing up in a rural area, I lived for trips to the library, where I would devour book after book, dominating the summer reading program. Back in my bedroom, I was transported to River Heights with Nancy Drew and Walnut Grove with Laura Ingalls. Though one was fictional and one was long since dead, both were very much alive in the pages of my books.

In high school, I worked at the library, indulging my OCD tendencies by cheerfully shelving books (oh, how I love you, Dewey decimal system) and helping other kids to read everything from Dr. Seuss to illustrated Shakespeare.

These days, I indulge my love of the written word by staying up all night and ruining my eyesight. It may be worth it (after all, books *are* available in Braille).

Be it high- or lowbrow, it matters not as long as the plot (along with my heart) races, the characters are juicy, and the writing soars. I'm equally entertained by Jane Austen's tart novels as I am by Diana Gabaldon's saucy, time-traveling, historical fiction *Outlander* series. Nonfiction ropes me in as well—I'll read the phone book if Malcolm Gladwell, Erik Larson, or Jon Krakauer are writing it. In fact, I won't put it down.

Because there's nothing better than when a classic takes you by surprise, or when a new release by your favorite author manages to wow you and cow you with one perfect *bon mot* after another. Books tether us to each other in the most wonderful of ways; I joined in when the world was collectively reading the last of the Harry Potter books. Imagine my delight when my Amazon delivery arrived that Saturday morning. Along with the rest of America, I canceled all other plans that weekend and hunkered down for a final visit with my favorite wizard.

Some are concerned about the state of publishing. Don't be.

The vehicle of delivery may change, but the ride will stay the same. As long as authors have something to say and unique ways of saying it, books are going nowhere and everywhere. Publishing is evolving. But our love affair with books—pulse-quickening plotlines, indelible characters, *words*—is as true as Katniss Everdeen's aim and as wide as the Sargasso Sea.

GRAND
OPENINGS

～～～～～～～

"In the beginning God
created the heavens
and the earth."

—*The Bible*

✒

"Call me Ishmael."

—*Moby-Dick,*
by Herman Melville

✒

"It is a truth universally acknowledged, that a single man in possession of a good fortune, must be in want of a wife."

—*Pride and Prejudice*,
by Jane Austen

"Happy families are all alike; every unhappy family is unhappy in its own way."

—*Anna Karenina*,
by Leo Tolstoy

"'Christmas won't be Christmas without any presents,' grumbled Jo, lying on the rug."

—*Little Women*,
by Louisa May Alcott

❧

"Amory Blaine inherited from his mother every trait, except the stray inexpressible few, that made him worth while."

—*This Side of Paradise*,
by F. Scott Fitzgerald

❧

"The stranger came early in February, one wintry day, through a biting wind and a driving snow, the last snowfall of the year, over the down, walking as it seemed from Bramblehurst railway station, and carrying a little black portmanteau in his thickly gloved hand."

—*The Invisible Man*, by H.G. Wells

❧

"For a long time, I went to bed early."

—*Swann's Way* from *In Search of Lost Time*, by Marcel Proust

"In a hole in the ground there lived a hobbit. Not a nasty, dirty, wet hole, filled with the ends of worms and an oozy smell, nor yet a dry, bare, sandy hole with nothing in it to sit down on or to eat: it was a hobbit-hole, and that means comfort."

—*The Hobbit,*
by J.R.R. Tolkien

"On the 24th of February, 1810, the look-out at Notre-Dame de la Garde signalled the three-master, the Pharaon from Smyrna, Trieste, and Naples."

—*The Count of Monte Cristo*,
by Alexandre Dumas

➤

"1801—I have just returned from a visit to my landlord—the solitary neighbor that I shall be troubled with."

—*Wuthering Heights*,
by Emily Brontë

➤

"Alice was beginning to get very tired of sitting by her sister on the riverbank, and of having nothing to do: once or twice she had peeped into the book her sister was reading, but it had no pictures or conversations in it, 'and what is the use of a book,' thought Alice, 'without pictures or conversation?'"

—*Alice's Adventures in Wonderland,*
by Lewis Carroll

"You will rejoice to hear that no disaster has accompanied the commencement of an enterprise which you have regarded with such evil forebodings."

—*Frankenstein*,
by Mary Shelley

"Ours is essentially a tragic age, so we refuse to take it tragically."

—*Lady Chatterley's Lover*,
by D.H. Lawrence

"Two households, both alike in dignity / In fair Verona, where we lay our scene / From ancient grudge break to new mutiny / Where civil blood makes civil hands unclean."

—*Romeo and Juliet,*
by William Shakespeare

"TRUE! - nervous - very, very dreadfully nervous I had been and am; but why will you say that I am mad?"

—*The Tell-Tale Heart,* by Edgar Allen Poe

"One may as well begin with Helen's letters to her sister."

—*Howard's End*, by E.M. Forster

"A throng of bearded men, in sad-colored garments and grey steeple-crowned hats, inter-mixed with women, some wearing hoods, and others bareheaded, was assembled in front of a wooden edifice, the door of which was heavily timbered with oak, and studded with iron spikes."

—*The Scarlet Letter*, by Nathaniel Hawthorne

"Don't get it right. Just get it written."

—JAMES THURBER

BEFORE THEY WERE
PUBLISHED, THESE BOOKS
WERE REJECTED WITH THE
FOLLOWING NOTATIONS.

The Great Gatsby, by F. Scott Fitzgerald:

"You'd have a decent book if you'd get rid of that
Gatsby character."

The Fountainhead, by Ayn Rand:

"I wish there were an audience for a book of this kind.
But there isn't. It won't sell."

BESTSELLERS THAT WERE REJECTED ... MANY TIMES

Jack Canfield and Mark Victor Hansen—*Chicken Soup for the Soul*—134

Robert Pirsig: *Zen and the Art of Motorcycle Maintenance*—121

Jasper Fforde, *The Eyre Affair*—76

Kathryn Stockett, *The Help*—60

Margaret Mitchell, *Gone with the Wind*—38

Dr. Seuss, *And to Think I Saw It on Mulberry Street*—27 rejections

Madeline L'Engle, *A Wrinkle in Time*—26

Audrey Niffenegger, *The Time Traveler's Wife*—25

William Golding, *Lord of the Flies*—20

Frank Herbert, *Dune*—20

Richard Bach, *Jonathan Livingston Seagull*—18

Anne Frank, *The Diary of Anne Frank*—15

e.e. cummings, *The Enormous Room*—15

John Grisham, *A Time to Kill*—16

J.K. Rowling, *Harry Potter and the Sorcerer's Stone*—12

Ayn Rand, *The Fountainhead*—12

Vladmir Nabokov, *Lolita*—5

My all-time favorite books:

Incunables *are books printed before 1501 and amongst the most prized possessions of modern libraries.*

THE MOST LITERATE
U.S. CITIES

2005:

Seattle, WA

2006:

Seattle, WA

2007:

Minneapolis, MN

2008:

Tie: Minneapolis, MN, and Seattle, WA

2009:

Seattle, WA

2010:

Washington, DC

Best books to plow through on a flight:

"In my writing I am acting as a mapmaker, an explorer of psychic areas, a cosmonaut of inner space, and I see no point in exploring areas that have already been thoroughly surveyed."

—WILLIAM S. BURROUGHS

FICTION'S PLUCKIEST HEROINES

Elizabeth Bennet

Flavia de Luce

Katniss Everdeen

Lisabeth Salander

Dorothy

Nancy Drew

Rosalind

Scarlett O'Hara

Lucy Honeychurch

"Practically everybody in New York

has half a mind

to write a book,

and does."

—GROUCHO MARX

FAMOUS GUMSHOES

Hercule Poirot

Kay Scarpetta

Adam Dalgliesh

Harry Hole

V.I. Warshawski

Thomas Lynley

Laughing Policeman Martin Beck

Matthew Skudder

The Hardy Boys

Jim Chee & Joe Leaphorn

"A book worth
reading is worth
buying."

—JOHN RUSKIN

The first line of the story of my life would be:

BELOVED BOOKS
ON WRITING

Bird by Bird,
by Anne Lamott

If You Want to Write,
by Brenda Ueland

On Writing,
by Stephen King

Stein on Writing,
by Sol Stein

Write Away,
by Elizabeth George

Writing the Breakout Novel,
by Donald Maass

Zen in the Art of Writing,
by Ray Bradbury

FICTION'S MOST DELICIOUS VILLAINS

Captain Hook

Clare Quilty

Count Dracula

Grendel's Mother

Hannibal Lecter

Iago

Kurtz

Lady Macbeth

Marquise de Merteuil

Moby-Dick

Moriarty

Mrs. Danvers

Patrick Bateman

President Snow

Roger Chillingworth

Sauron

The Volturi

The Wicked Witch of the West

Voldemort

"There is no such thing as
a moral or
an immoral book.
Books are well written,
or badly written."

—OSCAR WILDE

GOOD BOOKS
FOR BAD DAYS

Addiction:
A Million Little Pieces, by James Frey

All-around bad decision-making:
The House of Mirth, by Edith Wharton

Bad day at work:
Then We Came to the End, by Joshua Ferris.

Bad weather:
Krakatoa: The Day the World Exploded,
by Simon Winchester

Breakup:
High Fidelity, by Nick Hornby

Debt:
Confessions of a Shopaholic, by Sophie Kinsella

Depressed:
Prozac Nation, by Elizabeth Wurtzel

Divorce:
The War of the Roses, by Warren Adler

Inappropriate relationship:
Lolita, by Vladmir Nabokov

Fired:
Up in the Air, by Walter Kim

General ennui:
Catcher in the Rye, by J.D. Salinger

Grief:
The Year of Magical Thinking, by Joan Didion

Lovesickness:
Sense & Sensibility, by Jane Austen

Sick:
Terms of Endearment, by Larry McMurtry

Zombies:
The Passage, by Justin Cronin

A single Renaissance printing press could produce 3,600 pages per day. Previously, only 40 could be produced with typographic hand-printing.

My favorite childhood reads:

MAGICAL READS

The Physick Book of Deliverance Dane,
by Katherine Howe.
This literary mystery has a grad student tracking down
a book of spells and potions that date back to
the seventeenth century and personal ties
to the Salem witch trials.

The Witching Hour,
by Anne Rice.
The first of the Mayfair witches books,
The Witching Hour puts a Big Easy spin on witchcraft.
Neurosurgeon Rowan Mayfair discovers that she
comes from a long line of witches. Add to that an evil
spirit named Lasher eager to manifest in human form
and you've got a rollicking, Gothic tale with
a serious creep-out factor.

A Discovery of Witches,
by Deborah Harkness.
If a great dynasty witches isn't enough for you,
add in a literary mystery, time travel, and a dreamy
vampire for an altogether satisfying read.

"*Classic.*"

A book which people praise

and don't read."

—MARK TWAIN

"You cannot open a book without learning something."

—CONFUCIUS

FAMILY AFFAIRS

The Glass Castle,
by Jeannette Walls.
Read Walls' anguished childhood memoir about
growing up with less-than-stable parents—an
alcoholic father and free-spirited mother—and you'll
be filling your gratitude journal for your lot in life.

The Great Santini,
by Pat Conroy.
"One of the greatest gifts you can get as a writer is
to be born into an unhappy family," says Pat Conroy,
who clearly knows something about the subject by
the looks of this classic novel about a Marine
colonel who rules his family with an iron fist.

The Corrections,
by Jonathan Franzen.
With masterful attention to Midwestern detail,
Franzen tells a story of a family who, while gathering
for the holidays, has to face some harsh realities. This
National Book Award winner reminds us that "yes,
you can go home again. But you might not want to."

CHILDREN'S CLASSICS
FIT FOR ADULTS

The Wind in the Willows,
by Kenneth Graham.
Verbose animals work through their issues
with each other.

The Borrowers,
by Mary Norton.
Tiny folks have to borrow items from
"human beans" to get by.

A Wrinkle in Time,
by Madeleine L'Engle.
With the help of the tesseract, Meg and her friends
travel to strange lands to rescue Meg's dad.

The Phantom Tollbooth,
by Norton Juster.
Wordplay Gone Wonderful.

The Wonderful Wizard of Oz,
by Frank L. Baum.
Dorothy follows the yellow brick road to meet
the Wizard and get back to Kansas.

Alice's Adventures in Wonderland,
by Lewis Carroll.
Wackiness ensures when Alice goes
down the rabbit hole.

The Mouse and His Child,
by Russell Hoben.
The classic story of two toy mice and their quest
to become self-winding.

Charlotte's Web,
by E.B. White.
A spider saves a young pig from slaughter
in this Newbury Honor book.

"*A writer is someone for whom writing is more difficult than it is for other people.*"

—THOMAS MANN

CLASSIC SERIES
FOR GIRLS

Betsy-Tacy Books,
by Maud Hart Lovelace

Little House on the Prairie,
by Laura Ingalls Wilder

Nancy Drew Mystery Stories,
by Carolyn Keene

Pippi Longstocking,
by Astrid Lindgren

Trixie Belden,
by Julie Campbell

Books I will reread over and over:

"Jump, and you will
find out how to
unfold your wings
as you fall."

—RAY BRADBURY

"Maybe I was only then becoming aware of the weight, the inertia, the opacity of the world—qualities that stick to writing from the start, unless one finds some way of evading them."

—UMBERTO ECO

"Every burned
book enlightens
the world."

—RALPH WALDO EMERSON

DISHING IT UP:
A FEW FOOD MEMOIRS

Long Ago in France: My Years in Dijon,
by MFK Fisher.
Fisher recounts her years in the late 1920s and
early 30s in France as a newlywed.

Kitchen Confidential,
by Anthony Bourdain.
This chef and media personality chronicles everything
in the kitchen, talking about the difficulties of each
station, the excesses of chefs and staff, and why it's
not a good idea to order fish on Mondays.

Garlic and Sapphires,
by Ruth Reichl.
You'll eat up Reichl's memoir of her years
as the food critic—disguises and all—for
the *New York Times*.

The Sharper the Knife, the Less You Cry,
by Kathleen Flinn.
The author's forays and foibles at Le Cordon Bleu
are punctuated with a recipe in each chapter.
This American in Paris pursues her culinary
passions and discovers love in the process.

Blood, Bones & Butter,
by Gabrielle Hamilton.
"Blood, Bones, and Butter is, quite simply, the
far-and-away best chef or food-genre memoir... ever.
EVER." So says Anthony Bourdain.

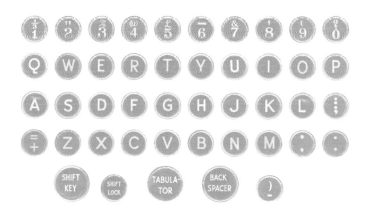

Bestselling series in history? Harry Potter, with 450 million books to date!

"Substitute 'damn' every time you're inclined to write 'very'; your editor will delete it and the writing will be just as it should be."

—MARK TWAIN

DYSTOPIAN READS

Nineteen Eighty-Four,
by George Orwell.
Big Brother is watching you in Oceania. Mind control
and government surveillance sounded slightly
implausible when the book was published in 1949,
but these Orwellian concepts were eerily prescient.

The Handmaid's Tale,
by Margaret Atwood.
The world has been taken over by men, and women
are stripped of their rights. Narrated by Offred,
a "handmaid" or concubine who is assigned to a
member of the ruling class to procreate, this chilling
version of the future explores themes relevant today.

The Children of Men,
by P.D. James.
What if the sperm count of all the men in the
human race plummeted to zero? How would
that change society? James explores these
questions in her gripping novel.

The Hunger Games,
by Suzanne Collins.
This may be shelved in the Young Adult section,
but you won't be able to put down this story of
a world where a lottery selects teens who
must fight to the death.

The Stand,
by Steven King.
You may be illin' but at least you're not one of
the few people who are mysteriously unaffected by
a biological weapon that has wiped out the rest
of humanity in King's 1,000-plus-page saga.

The most expensive book ever sold was the Codex Leicester, a 72-page notebook of writings and sketches of Leonardo da Vinci. Bill Gates purchased the book in 1994 for $30.8 million.

Epic novels I was sad to finish:

"A writer is congenitally unable to tell the truth and that is why we call what he writes fiction."

—MOLIÈRE

Books I will reread over and over:

LOVE HURTS

Romeo & Juliet,
by William Shakespeare.
The granddaddy of all tragic love stories,
just try not to weep when you revisit the story
of these star-crossed lovers from Verona.
"For never was a story of more woe / Than this
of Juliet and her Romeo." Verily.

Jane Eyre,
by Charlotte Bronte.
After growing up in a cold orphanage, Jane Eyre takes
a post as governess at Thornfield, only to fall for her
brooding employer Mr. Rochester, who has a secret
that could destroy more than just their love.

Revolutionary Road,
by Richard Yates.
Married with children and living in a nice Connecticut
suburb, the Wheelers seem to be living the American
dream. But they want more out of life, even
though they aren't sure what that is, which leads
to serious discontent.

The Age of Innocence,
by Edith Wharton.
The 1870s world that Wharton describes is lovely,
certainly, but it's also full of societal conventions and
constraints. This is bad news for Newland Archer,
engaged to be married but in love with his
fiancée's married cousin.

The English Patient,
by Michael Ondaatje.
A scorching World War II affair between a married
Brit and a desert explorer ends badly, but this
sweeping novel just might have you reading
Herodotus as fiery foreplay.

"The art of writing is the art of discovering what you believe."

—GUSTAVE FLAUBERT

"Ass in chair."

—NORA EPHRON

10 BOOKS FROM HIGH SCHOOL YOU REALLY SHOULD REVISIT

1.

Frankenstein, by Mary Shelley.
The classic cautionary tale that touches on themes
of man vs. science, man vs. nature, and man vs. God.
It's the whole monster enchilada.

2.

The Scarlet Letter, by Nathaniel Hawthorne.
Hester Prynne raises her daughter in a small
Puritanical community, refusing to reveal the name of
her lover, despite the fact that her long-lost husband
Roger Chillingworth shows up wanting to exact
psychological revenge.

3.

The Catcher in the Rye, by J.D. Salinger.
The most censored book in U.S. high schools between
1961 and 1982 is at its heart a story of modern-

day alienation and ennui. Original emo boy Holden
Caulfield is expelled from prep school and heads
for Manhattan, where he feels utterly alone and
misunderstood.

4.

The Great Gatsby, by F. Scott Fitzgerald.
One of the great American novels about the American
dream, Fitzgerald's masterpiece is the story of
Jay Gatsby, a self-made man who moves to Long
Island to impress and woo back his lost love Daisy.
Things don't exactly go as planned.

5.

Pride & Prejudice, by Jane Austen.
This tart and tasty bonbon of manners and courtship
centers around Elizabeth Bennet and her sisters,
as her mother clumsily attempts to make a good
match for them. When Mr. Darcy arrives in Meryton
with his fortune and snooty airs, Elizabeth isn't
impressed. But just wait.

6.

Siddhartha, by Herman Hesse.
Hesse's story, about the spiritual journey of a man who
lived at the time of the Buddha, offers up inspiration
in your search to be one with everything.

7.

Lord of the Flies, by William Golding.
Golding's novel is chilling, showing how easily
society can unravel. You'll be shaken to your core,
and you'll never look at a conch shell quite
the same way again.

8.

The Adventures of Huckleberry Finn,
by Mark Twain.
Huck hits the road, or in this case, the Mississippi
River to escape an abusive drunkard of a dad.
He meets up with runaway slave Jim, and the two
of them embark on a journey along the river.

9.

To Kill a Mockingbird, by Harper Lee.
Told through the eyes of young Scout Finch,
Mockingbird centers around a wrongly accused
black man on trial for rape and the barely latent
prejudices that surface during the court case.
But it's so much more.

10.

The Fountainhead, by Ayn Rand.
Rand always sparks a lot of controversy for her
Objectivist philosophy, but this story of Frank Lloyd
Wright–like architect Howard Roark is a testament
to absolute vision and belief in oneself. Rather than
compromise, Roark again and again refuses to
dull his shine, collaborate, or otherwise give in,
no matter the consequences.

Guilty pleasure books that I'm afraid to admit that I love:

"*Writing is like*
prostitution.
First you do it for love, and
then for a few
close friends,
and then for money."

—WILLIAM FAULKNER

GUILTY
PLEASURES

Outlander,
by Diane Gabaldon.
Time travel meets historical fiction meets undying
love. English nurse Claire Randall walks through
some stones in the Scottish highlands and finds
herself transported to 1743, where she meets
strapping redheaded Jamie Fraser. Yum.

Shanna,
by Kathleen Woodiwiss.
The classic bodice-ripper, you'll swoon over hunky
Ruark Beauchamp and his passion for headstrong,
beautiful Shanna. To prevent marrying a man of
her father's choosing, our heroine gets hitched to a
man headed to the hangman's noose. He, of course,
shakes off the rope and shows up at her Caribbean
island home, where love blossoms like a lush,
blooming hibiscus.

The Clan of the Cave Bear,
by Jean M. Auel.
Orphaned Cro-Magnon Ayla is adopted by a clan
of Neanderthals. As one of the "Others," her brain
and body work differently, which her new tribe
isn't exactly thrilled about.

Flowers in the Attic,
by V.C. Andrews.
Get your creep on and delve into the world of the
Dollanganger children, four gorgeous blond siblings
who seem to have it all, until their dad dies and they
wind up locked in the attic of their grandmother's
mansion. Mom is hiding them so she can get a fresh
start in society, and grandma dearest considers
them the devil's spawn.

The DaVinci Code,
by Dan Brown.
Who doesn't love a good mystery, especially one that
calls into question the history of the Western world?
Join symbologist Robert Langdon and cryptographer
Sophie Neveu on their breathless quest for
the Holy Grail. Godspeed.

"I try to leave out the parts that people skip."

—ELMORE LEONARD

If I chose a *nom de plume* and could write anonymously, I would be known in literary circles as:

And I would write about:

VIVE LA FRANCE!

A Moveable Feast,
by Ernest Hemingway.
Hemingway + Fitzgerald + Paris + drinking + roadtrip
= literary classic.

The Paris Wife,
by Paula McLain.
McLain writes a beautiful, fictionalized take on the
love affair between Hemingway and his first wife
Hadley. A great companion to *A Moveable Feast.*

Me Talk Pretty One Day,
by David Sedaris.
Humorist Sedaris takes his show on the road, moving
to France with his long-suffering partner Hugh.
Sedaris is a *poisson* out of water and chronicles
all of the good, bad, and hilarious.

A Year in Provence,
by Peter Mayle.
A British ad exec trades in his busy London life for
a 200-year-old fixer-upper in the south of France.
As each month passes, Mayle learns the delights
of rustic regional cuisine and the frustrations
of the locals' work schedule.

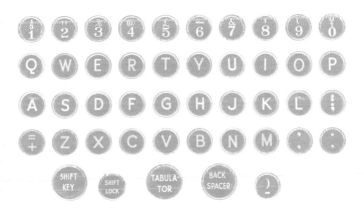

"Writing is
nothing more
than a guided
dream."

—JORGE LUIS BORGES

Books I've lent to people that I'm dying to get back:

SCIENCE IS FUN!

The Beak of the Finch,
by Jonathan Weiner.
Darwinism is experienced in real time as Weiner
chronicles the work of Peter and Rosemary Grant,
who observe Galapagos finches evolve in just
a few generations.

The Emperor of Scent,
by Chandler Burr.
Luca Turin, a darling and enfant terrible in the
perfume industry, puts forth a new theory about how
we smell (vibrations!) and sets about proving it with
cutting-edge technology. Burr explains Turin's quest
in the most compelling of ways.

Longitude,
by Dava Sobel.
We take time for granted, but once upon a time,
the greatest minds in the world couldn't figure out how
to keep accurate time... until a humble watchmaker
came along and created a timepiece that could
keep precise time at sea.

The Immortal Life of Henrietta Lacks,
by Rebecca Skloot.
Known as HeLa to scientists, Lacks was a poor black
woman whose cells—taken unbeknownst to her—have
been grown in culture, helping to create the polio
vaccine, uncover secrets of cancer, and aid in cloning
and gene mapping. Buried in an unmarked grave,
Lacks may well be the most important person
who ever lived.

Isaac's Storm,
by Erik Larson.
Journalist Erik Larson kicked off his literary career
with a bang with this true tale about the beginnings
of the National Weather Service and a hurricane
that rocked Galveston in 1900.

"One must be an inventor to read well.There is creative reading as well as creative writing."

—RALPH WALDO EMERSON

"When I have a little money,
I buy books.
If any is left over, I buy
food and clothes."

—DESIDERIUS ERASMUS

"The only thing to be said this time about *Fear & Loathing* is that it was fun to write and that's fair, for me at least because I've always considered writing the most hateful kind of work."

—HUNTER S. THOMPSON

Invented by goldsmith Johannes Gutenberg circa 1440, the printing press revolutionized publishing.

TRAGIC-COMIC READS

Bridget Jones' Diary,
by Helen Fielding.
Spawning a whole genre of "chick lit," Fielding's
novel is a hilarious take on singleton Bridget as she
navigates crap jobs, weight fluctuations, and suitors
of the nightmare and dreamboat variety.

A Confederacy of Dunces,
by John Kennedy Toole.
There's never been a protagonist quite like Ignatius J.
Reilly. A legend in his own mind, he pontificates and
bungles his way through various jobs in New Orleans,
a modern Don Quixote of sorts.

Talking to Girls about Duran Duran,
by Rob Sheffield.
Be transported back to the 1980s, in all its New Wave,
neon, wildly awkward, adolescent glory in Sheffield's
hilarious memoir. Let the dulcet tones of
Simon Le Bon heal what ails you.

Bossypants,
by Tina Fey.
Fey is never afraid to use herself and her own life to
mine comic gold and to make a statement on modern
culture. In her hilarious memoir, she offers a pastiche
of her memories, jokes, skits, and scripts, taking
us behind the scenes and inside the mind of
TV's reigning queen of comedy.

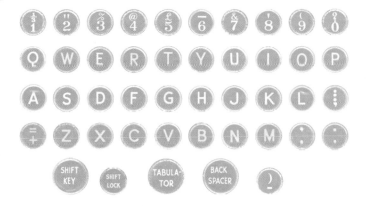

THE SPORTING LIFE

Wait Till Next Year,
Doris Kearns Goodwin.
Goodwin as a Dodgers fan in 1950s New York. This
sweet memoir captures both the era and her childhood
through the joy of America's pastime.

Moneyball,
by Michael Lewis.
Professional sports is big business, but not all teams'
payrolls are created equal. Lewis follows the
low-payroll Oakland A's as their general manager
Billy Beane transforms how a team is built and
creates a winning formula in the process.

True Believers,
by Joe Queenan.
Satirist Joe Queenan turns his jaundiced eye toward
the wind beneath a team's wings: the fans. Traveling
around the country, Queenan looks at various college
and pro sports fans and attempts to get at what
drives their fanaticism.

Seabiscuit,
by Laura Hillenbrand.
By all accounts, Seabiscuit shouldn't have been
a champion. But this gripping, better-than-fiction
story details the millionaire, the mustang breaker,
and red-headed jockey who put their bets
on this racehorse.

"A book must
be an axe for
the frozen sea
within us."

—KAFKA

"The worst thing about new books is that they keep us from reading the old ones."

—JOHN WOODEN

LITERARY LOVE

Another Life,
by Michael Korda.
With forty-one years in publishing, Korda certainly
has some good stories to tell, and he shares them
here in delicious, spot-on detail.

The Book of Air and Shadows,
by Michael Gruber.
What if Shakespeare wrote one more play, one that's
been hidden for hundreds of years? This is the
premise of Gruber's bibliophilic thriller.

Book Business,
by Jason Epstein.
With a storied career in the publishing industry,
Epstein is the perfect person to guide the reader
through the industry—past, present, and
the ever-evolving future.

The Shadow of the Wind,
by Carlos Ruiz Zafón.
Daniel Sempere is living in 1950s Barcelona when
he's taken to The Cemetery of Lost Books and allowed
to pick out one book of the labyrinth of shelves.
The book he chooses, *The Shadow of the Wind,*
sets him on a mystery filled with intrigue,
love, and maybe even the devil.

The Book Thief,
by Markus Zusak.
Meet Liesel, a foster child in World War II Germany
who can't resist stealing books and sharing them with
neighbors during mankind's darkest days.

> "*Write drunk,*
>
> *edit sober.*"

—ERNEST HEMINGWAY

Bestselling single-volume book in history? A Tale of Two Cities, by Charles Dickens, with 200 million copies.

UP ALL NIGHT:
SCARY READS

Jaws,
by Peter Benchley.
The perfect beach read, Benchley's tale of
a great white shark terrorizing vacationers
on Amity Island will make you never
want to go into the water again.

The Snowman,
by Jo Nesbo.
If you like *The Girl with the Dragon Tattoo,*
you won't be able to put down the story of
a serial killer who leaves a snowman as his
calling card and the brilliant alcoholic cop
who tracks him down.

The Alienist,
by Caleb Carr.
Be transported back to turn-of-the-century New York,
in this gripping tale of a serial killer and the motley
group that uses psychology to track him down.

Carrie,
by Stephen King.
A list of scary books wouldn't be complete without one
of King's classics. Carrie is a shy teen who discovers
she has telekinetic powers; it's not long before she's
using them to wreak havoc on her tormentors.
Oh, and her mother's a piece of work.

Red Dragon,
by Thomas Harris.
The book that introduced the world to Hannibal
Lecter, *Red Dragon* is also unputdownable for
the detailed FBI hunt for a creepy killer.

"I am the literary
equivalent of a Big
Mac and fries."

—STEPHEN KING

Novels so scary that they curled by toes:

LITERARY
MYSTERIES

The Historian,
by Elizabeth Kostova.
A scholar disappears from his office, with only
an ancient book left behind as a clue. This leads his
daughter on a search for him and the truth that takes
her to Istanbul, Budapest, and beyond, uncovering
the truth about Dracula in the process.

Ghostwalk,
by Rebecca Stott.
Cambridge, a mysterious death, Isaac Newton,
alchemy, a ghost or two—what's not to like?
When a Cambridge scholar is found drowned,
another academic goes about trying to finish
her revelatory biography of Isaac Newton, and
in the process, finds links between a series
of seventeenth-century murders and a rash
of current-day killings.

The Rule of Four,
by Ian Caldwell and Dustin Thomason.
Four roommates, all set to graduate, get sucked into
trying to solve a puzzling Renaissance text, all the
while dodging other academics eager to get their
ambitious hands on the solution.

The Dante Club,
by Matthew Pearl.
When a rash of murders inspired by Dante's Inferno
break out in 1865 Boston, who better than Longfellow,
Oliver Wendell Holmes, James Russell Lowell,
and J.T. Fields to solve it?

SHORT STORIES

What We Talk About When We Talk About Love,
by Raymond Carver.
Carver sets the bar for gut-wrenching,
human short stories in this collection.

The Things They Carried,
by Tim O'Brien.
The title story is oft discussed in English classes for
its perfection, a story about Vietnam soldiers as told
through the belongings they bring with them to war.

Come to Me,
by Amy Bloom.
This 1993 collection explores love in its many
glorious, dysfunctional, and unlikely forms. And
it always rings true, thanks to Bloom's career
as a psychotherapist.

Runaway,
Alice Munro.
Munro continually puts out amazing short stories
about the human condition through the lens of daily
life. Get to know her mastery through this
Giller Prize–winning collection.

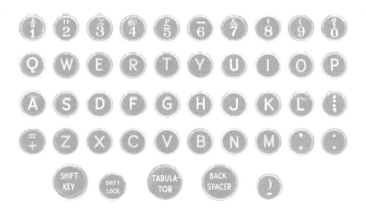

"My perfect day is sitting in a room with some blank paper. That's heaven. That's gold and anything else is just a waste of time."

—CORMAC MCCARTHY

Books I couldn't put down:

Romance novels that made me swoon:

"It took me fifteen years to discover that I had no talent for writing, but I couldn't give it up because by that time I was too famous."

—ROBERT BENCHLEY

Books that are literary Ambien, always putting me to sleep:

"In certain kinds of writing, particularly in art criticism and literary criticism, it is normal to come across long passages which are almost completely lacking in meaning."

—GEORGE ORWELL

*The Gutenberg Bible,
the first book ever printed
with moveable type, was
created in 1456. Twenty-one
are believed to be completely
intact and are valued at
up to $35 million.*

ROAD TRIPPIN'

On the Road,
by Jack Kerouac.
The nonstop driving of Sal and Dean as they
crisscross North America mirrors Kerouac's
own Beat writing jag.

Into the Wild,
by Jon Krakauer.
A young man's search for meaning leads him to
an isolated, abandoned bus in Alaska.

The Adventures of Huckleberry Finn,
by Mark Twain.
An American Odyssey, Huck and runaway slave
Jim travel throughout the South, meeting and
dodging all sorts of unsavory characters.

TRUE ADVENTURE

A Perfect Storm,
by Sebastian Junger.
Junger does a masterful job telling the story of the
doomed *Andrea Gail* and its crew, filling in the blanks
with interviews and intelligent supposition.

Into Thin Air,
by Jon Krakauer.
Climbing Mount Everest is a challenge even
with perfect conditions, but when things go wrong
on the mountain, they go really, really wrong,
as Krakauer recounts in this gripping true story
of mountaineering tragedy.

Into the Heart of the Sea,
by Nathaniel Philbrick.
The story that inspired Moby Dick, this whale
of a tale chronicles a rogue whale attack that
destroyed a whaling ship, leaving sailors adrift
and forced to face some grim choices.

The first edition of Shakespeare's plays was published in 1623. There are 228 remaining copies of the First Folio; they are valued upwards of $20 million.

"Either write
something worth
reading or
do something
worth writing."

—BENJAMIN FRANKLIN

Lines from books that were so good they stopped me in my tracks:

TRUE CRIME

In Cold Blood,
by Truman Capote.
Capote changed the face of journalism with
this chilling "non-fiction novel" about a pair
of killers in 1959 Kansas farm country.

The Monster of Florence,
by Douglas Preston.
A serial killer stalked young lovers in the Tuscan
hills between 1968 and 1985; this book details
the search for the killer's identity.

Zodiac,
by Robert Graysmith.
A cartoonist working for the *San Francisco Chronicle*
when the Zodiac murders started, Graysmith
transformed his obsession with the unsolved crimes
into this compelling book.

The Devil in the White City,
by Erik Larson.
Discover how the Chicago World's Fair came to be—
in a narrative interwoven with the story of
a baby-faced serial killer.

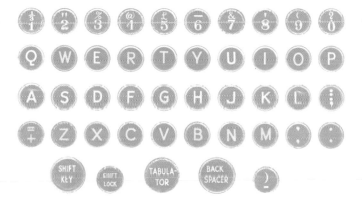

"I've never known any trouble that an hour's reading didn't assuage."

—ARTHUR SCHOPENHAUER

Endings of books that surprised me:

THE LAST
WORD

~~~~~~~~~

"I'm so glad to be
at home again."

—*The Wonderful Wizard of Oz,* by L. Frank Baum

✒

"He was soon borne away by
the waves and lost in darkness
and distance."

—*Frankenstein,* by Mary Shelley

✒

"And so, as Tiny Tim observed, God bless Us, Every One!"

—*A Christmas Carol,*
by Charles Dickens

"But, in spite of these deficiencies, the wishes, the hopes, the confidence, the predictions of the small band of true friends who witnessed the ceremony, were fully answered in the happiness of the union."

—*Emma,* by Jane Austen

"All that is very well," answered Candide, "but let us cultivate our garden."

—*Candide*, by Voltaire

"There was the hum of bees, and the musky odor of pinks filled the air."

—*The Awakening*, by Kate Chopin

"It was not till they had examined the rings that they recognized who it was."

—*The Picture of Dorian Gray*, by Oscar Wilde

"So we beat on, boats against the current, borne back ceaselessly into the past."

—*The Great Gatsby*, by F. Scott Fitzgerald

"At that, as if it had been the signal he waited for, Newland Archer got up slowly and walked back alone to his hotel."

—*The Age of Innocence*, by Edith Wharton

"As soon as they had strength they arose, joined hands again, and went on."

—*Tess of the d'Urbervilles*, by Thomas Hardy

"That might be the subject of a new story, but our present story is ended."

—*Crime and Punishment*,
by Fyodor Dostoevsky

❧

"Come, children, let us shut up the box and the puppets, for our play is played out."

—*Vanity Fair*,
by William Makepeace Thackeray

❧

"He knelt by the bed and bent over her, draining their last moment to its lees; and in the silence there passed between them the word which made all clear."

—*The House of Mirth,*
by Edith Wharton

***

"Ah Bartleby! Ah humanity!"

—*Bartleby the Scrivener,*
by Herman Melville

"If the doctor told me I had six minutes to live I'd type a little faster."

—ISAAC ASIMOV

ABOUT THE AUTHOR

Jennifer Worick is the co-author of the *New York Times* bestseller *The Worst-Case Scenario Survival Handbook: Dating & Sex* as well as *The Worst-Case Scenario Survival Handbook: College*. In addition, she is the author or co-author of more than 25 hilarious and helpful books, including *Nancy Drew's Guide to Life, The Prairie Girl's Guide to Life, Simple Gifts, Backcountry Betty,* and *The Action Heroine's Handbook*. Jennifer is a publishing consultant, a regular books contributor to today.com, and a humorous blogger (jenniferworick.blogspot.com). And, oh yeah, she loves books.

ABOUT CIDER MILL PRESS
BOOK PUBLISHERS

Good ideas ripen with time. From seed to harvest,
Cider Mill Press brings fine reading, information,
and entertainment together between the covers of its
creatively crafted books. Our Cider Mill bears fruit
twice a year, publishing a new crop of titles each
spring and fall.

*Where Good Books Are
Ready for Press*

Visit us on the web at
www.cidermillpress.com
or write to us at
12 Port Farm Road
Kennebunkport, Maine 04046